TOP CLASS

Punctuation

Year 4

Now supported with CPD training
For info visit www.johnmurraycpd.co.uk

John Murray

Published by Hopscotch, a division of MA Education, St Jude's Church, Dulwich Road, London, SE24 0PB
www.hopscotchbooks.com
020 7738 5454

©2015 MA Education Ltd

Written by John Murray

Series designed by Claire White,
Fonthill Creative, 01722 717029

Illustrations by Emma Turner and Sara Cullen

Associate Publisher: Angela Morano Shaw

ISBN 9781909860186

All rights reserved. This resource is sold subject to the condition that it shall not, by way of trade or otherwise, be lent, hired out or otherwise circulated without the publisher's prior consent in any form of binding or cover other than that in which it is published and without a similar condition, including this condition, being imposed upon the subsequent purchaser.

No part of this publication may be reproduced, stored in a retrieval system, or transmitted, in any form or by any means, electronic, mechanical, photocopying, recording or otherwise, without the prior permission of the publisher, except where photocopying for educational purposes within the school or other educational establishment that has purchased this book is expressly permitted in the text.

Every effort has been made to trace the owners of copyright of material in this book and the publisher apologises for any inadvertent omissions. Any persons claiming copyright for any material should contact the publisher who will be happy to pay the permission fees agreed between them and who will amend the information in this book on any subsequent reprint.

Contents Page

Introduction 6

Capital Letters 8

Full Stops 12

Question Marks 16

Exclamation Marks 20

Commas I (within lists) 24

Commas II (within clauses) 28

Inverted Commas 32

Apostrophes (for omission) 36

Apostrophes (for possession) 40

Brackets 44

Ellipses 48

Colons 52

Semi-colons 56

Punctuation for Parenthesis 60

Introduction

Top Class is a series that endeavours to combine traditional approaches to the teaching and learning of grammar, punctuation and vocabulary with new techniques and activities that support and encourage good learning.

The three core areas have been separated into three distinct books aimed primarily at Key Stage 2. The three books ought to be used in conjunction with each other in order to provide learners with a wider learning environment and for them to understand that these core elements of Literacy work together and are not to be applied in isolation.

Specific elements of the new Key Stage 3 National Curriculum have also been included in order to introduce Key Stage 2 learners to more complex grammatical constructions and vocabulary as they make their transition from attaining Level 4 to Level 5 in writing.

Each book, one for each Year group in Key Stage 2, aims to promote discussion about specific areas of Literacy and provide experiences and opportunities to use and apply what they have learnt.

The three books are as follows:

- **Top Class – Grammar**
- **Top Class – Punctuation**
- **Top Class – Vocabulary**

Each book contains lessons that develop a 'top-down' approach, allowing learners to see how we use language in context, not simply *when* we use a particular word, punctuation mark or grammatical construct but *how* to use it to its best effect when writing independently.

As such, it actively promotes the core principle that to learn grammar and punctuation well and to extend your personal vocabulary effectively, then you must not only see these particular elements of Literacy within authentic and meaningful context and settings but you must then have the opportunity to apply what you have understood in your own independent writing.

All too often children are taught grammar, punctuation and vocabulary with exercises that aren't rooted within an authentic experience; and, as a result, although they may gain full marks in their exercise books, they often misapply or omit what has been learnt in their own free writing.

The *Top Class* series seeks to address this problem using a three staged approach, each Lesson Plan being structured so that learners are encouraged to investigate and explore the English language; initially with support and guidance from their teacher and fellow peers before being asked to apply what they have learnt as individuals.

Think about...

Before undertaking the Guided activity, learners are asked about what they already know about a particular piece of punctuation or grammatical form and where they might have seen it.

This links directly to the Guided text, again helping learners to view grammar, punctuation and vocabulary in context, housing it so that stronger links can be made with prior learning and personal experiences. This can then be used as a springboard to explore and develop this further in a familiar setting.

For example, when looking at our use of capital letters when writing a proper noun, learners may be asked about why people use an atlas or map before looking at a tourist map of London and considering why place names and famous tourist attractions start with a capital letter.

Guided

This is a shared activity that engages the whole class.

Set within a specific and relevant genre of Literacy, it embeds each particular piece of grammar, punctuation or vocabulary being taught in a focused and meaningful way. Moreover, it invites learners to use this information in order to answer a series of questions that are related to the text itself and then begins to move beyond it.

Each of the three questions asked have been carefully formatted so that valuable practice for the end of *Key Stage 2 English grammar, punctuation and spelling test* can be undertaken throughout each Year group. Marks are also available so that pupils gain practice at providing fuller explanations for those questions where two or three marks are being awarded. Answers are provided on the Lesson Plan.

Independent

This activity can be completed as an individual, with a partner or within a small group.

Each Independent activity within the book is also differentiated at an upper and lower level* and offers teachers a range of practical activities that support learners as they practice what they have learnt in the Guided section.

Differentiated activities can be found on the CD Rom.

Homework

Included in this section is a homework activity that aims to encourage wider learning outside of the classroom to take place. There are two types of homework activities that are provided, each having been designed to help learners discover and engage with grammar, punctuation and vocabulary in the 'real' world:

A] Specific 'closed' questions may be asked in order that research skills, both modern and traditional, can be employed to find a particular answer.

For example: What is the capital city of Demark? Who was the first man to walk on the moon? When necessary, answers are provided on the Lesson Plan.

B] Wider 'open' tasks are given in order to afford learners the opportunity to explore the world around them and collect examples that are both pertinent and authentic.

For example, learners may be asked to find three examples where a shop's name uses an **apostrophe in their local** high street.

Extension

This final stage of the learning journey is an important one and underscores the importance of using a 'top-down' approach to the teaching and learning of grammar, punctuation and vocabulary.

Each Extension activity within the book is also differentiated at an upper and lower level.*

Its aim is to encourage children to apply what they have learnt in a meaningful and purposeful way in order to embed their learning.

For example, learners may be asked to write a shopping list when planning a party that will naturally include a colon or use strong adjectives to describe a certain event in a story.

More importantly, it is this *writing for purpose* (rather than to score arbitrary marks or achieve irrelevant ticks in an exercise book) that provides a meaningful opportunity for individuals to engage with the English language and create their own work that uses grammar, punctuation and vocabulary in a way that brings their work to life.

In this way, not only will each learner be encouraged to use particular forms of grammar, punctuation or vocabulary correctly but, essentially, they will gain a strong sense of themselves taking an active role as a writer. It gives them a valuable sense of what it is like to be an author, one who uses grammar not only to improve the quality of their work but also to express themselves as best they can using the written word.

The journey from simply understanding how the English language works to being able to apply that knowledge in order to become a capable and confident writer is a journey that will continue into adulthood and one that, in all truthfulness, never really ends.

However, by providing meaningful activities for both the classroom and beyond, the *Top Class* series can help each and every writer to freely use grammar, punctuation and vocabulary to great effect and support them as they endeavour to bring the written word to life in order to inform, influence and entertain their readers.

Differentiated activities can be found on the CD Rom.

Capital Letters

Think about...
Why do people use an atlas or a map?
Who might want to look at a map of London?
Why do place names start with a capital letter?
What other places on a map would start with a capital?
Why?

Guided

Imagine you are a tourist visiting London for the first time.

What might you want to see? With a partner, choose three places to go and visit and plan a route that will help you explore them.

Once done, share your plan with another group and discuss why you would like to go there. Then answer the questions on page 9.

Independent

Use a UK atlas to find other places you would like to visit.

On your own, with a partner or in a small group; complete the task sheet provided to you by your teacher on page 10.

Once finished, cut off the homework task to take home with you for further practice.

Extension

Write a report describing the people and places of a new island that you discover. Complete the task sheet on page 11.

Once completed, draw and label a map of the island itself!

Answers

1. The River Thames

2. Big Ben

3. We walked over <u>T</u>ower <u>B</u>ridge towards <u>B</u>uckingham <u>P</u>alace.

Homework

- Copenhagen
- The River Yangtze
- Lake Victoria
- Rhode Island

Remember...
We use **capital letters** to start the names of people and important places but also for rivers, lakes and mountains.

Capital Letters

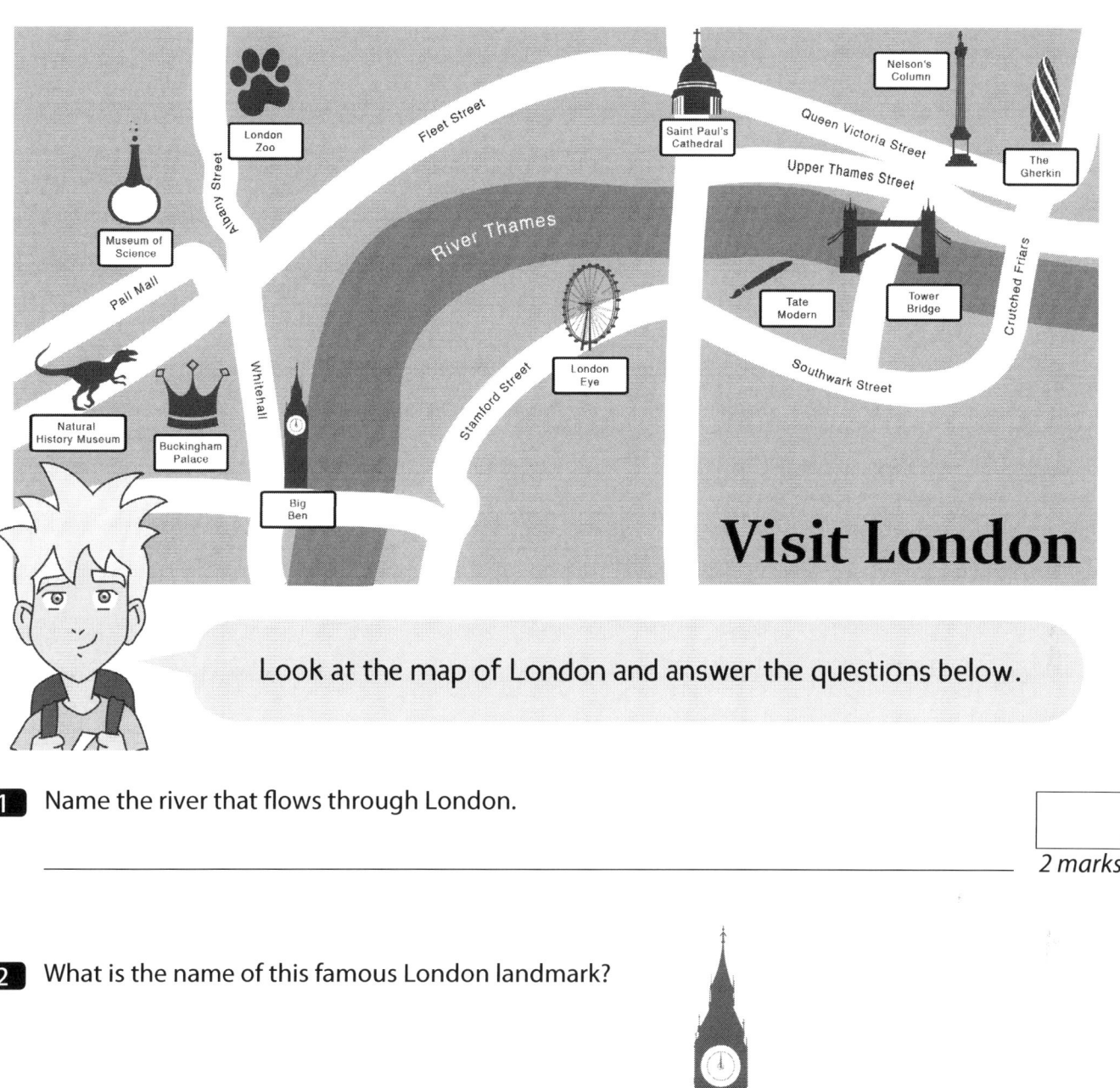

Look at the map of London and answer the questions below.

1 Name the river that flows through London.

_____ 2 marks

2 What is the name of this famous London landmark?

_____ 1 mark

3 Underline the words that should start with a capital letter.

We walked over tower bridge towards buckingham palace.

Why do these words need a capital letter?

_____ 3 marks

Capital Letters

Use a UK atlas to find where you live or somewhere you would like to visit. Make a list of five places for each of the boxes below. Don't forget to use a capital letter to start each of your examples.

Towns	Cities
Rivers	**Parks**
Lakes	**Mountains**

Homework

Use a world atlas to find the following:
- The capital city of Denmark
- The longest river in China
- The biggest lake in Africa
- The smallest state of America

Capital Letters

You discover a new island! Write a report about the people and places that you find on this strange new land. What is it called? Who lives there? What are its major cities and places of interest? Why would others want to go there?

| **Name:** | **Date:** |

Island:

Discovery Date:

Location:

Population:

TOP CLASS - Punctuation - Year 4

Full Stops

Think about...
Do you know what a phoenix is?
What do you already know about this mythical bird?
What would you like to know about it?
How might you research this to find your answers?

Guided

Imagine you are asked to look up some information on the phoenix.

What questions might someone like to ask about it? Why? With a partner, list three questions you would like to ask about the phoenix and think of three ways in which you might find the answer to your questions. What might the answer to each question be?

Once done, find another pair and compare your questions and possible answers. Then answer the questions on page 13.

Independent

Find out about an ancient Greek monster.

On your own, with a partner or in a small group; complete the task sheet provided to you by your teacher on page 14.

Once finished, cut off the homework task to take home with you for further practice.

Extension

Write a short story about when you battle against your ancient Greek monster. Complete the task sheet on page 15.

Once written, practice reading your story out loud to a friend; acting it out with your voice so that your story comes alive!

Answers

1  | 1 | 2 | 3 | 4 | 5 |

2 I. It is the end of a sentence.

II. The next line begins with a capital letter even though it is not a name.

3

Statement of Truth	Statement of Opinion
A	B
C	D

Homework

- Perseus killed Medusa
- Theseus killed the Minotaur
- Odysseus killed the Cyclops Polyphemus
- Heracles killed Nessus

Remember...
We use a **full stop** to mark the end of a sentence.

Full Stops

www.ancientgreekmyths.com   The Phoenix

The Legend of the Phoenix

The phoenix is one of the most famous birds in Greek mythology

With eyes as blue as sapphires and with a plumage of royal purple and crimson red, with legs scaled with gold and adorned with rose-colored talons, its vibrancy was one to behold.

Living for a thousand years, as the sun began to set on a lifetime of adventures, it would begin to build its own funeral pyre Once built (and before its dying breath) the pyre was lit and this magical creature would throw itself into the burning inferno.

Soon the dawning of a new life would begin; the phoenix being born anew, rising from the ashes to live its next millennium.

In alternative versions of the legend, its final act would be to lay a single egg within the glowing embers, which would then hatch into a new phoenix...a continuous life cycle for a supernatural beast.

Look at this web page and answer the questions below.

1 Which two paragraphs are missing a full stop?

> 1   2   3   4   5

2 marks

2 What clues helped you find your answers?

I. _____

II. _____

1 mark

3 Fill in the table below.

Statement of Truth	Statement of Opinion

A) **According to the legend, the phoenix lived for a thousand years.**

B) **The phoenix looked beautiful.**

C) **The phoenix is a mythological bird.**

D) **To see a phoenix reborn would be amazing.**

3 marks

Full Stops

Look up some information about an ancient Greek monster of your choice. Draw a picture of your mythical beast and write a Fact File about it. Don't forget to put a full stop at the end of each sentence.

Fact File:

Where did it live?

What did it look like?

What did it eat?

Did it have any special powers?

Who killed it?

Homework

Who killed the following Greek monsters?
- Medusa
- The Minotaur
- The Cyclops Polyphemus
- Nessus

Full Stops

You are ready to do battle with an ancient Greek monster. Use the research you have completed for your Fact File to help you. Where will your story be set? Why do you want to kill this mythical beast? How will you do so?

Name: **Date:**

The sun beat down, cold beads of sweat trickling down my neck...there was no going back. Without another word, I took one last breath and walked deep into the cool dark shadow beyond.

TOP CLASS - Punctuation - Year 4

Question Marks

Think about...
Why do people tell jokes?
Why do certain jokes keep to a particular format? (Doctor, Doctor or Knock, Knock jokes)
What do you notice about these two types of jokes?
Why do you think both these types of jokes use a question?

Guided

Imagine you are a stand up comic.

Write down your favourite joke. Why is your joke funny? Practice telling your joke inside your head. How would you use your voice when saying it out loud? Which words would you stress? When would you pause and for how long? How would you deliver the punch line?

Once done, walk around the class telling your joke and listening to how others tell theirs. How many of the jokes you hear contain a question? Then answer the questions on page 17.

Independent

You are a comedian and are putting together a new stand up routine.

On your own, with a partner or in a small group; complete the task sheet provided to you by your teacher on page 18.

Once finished, cut off the homework task to take home with you for further practice.

Extension

Create a joke board. Complete the task sheet on page 19.

Once completed, find a partner and practice your jokes on them.

Answers

1

Question	Doctor	Patient
Are you choking?	✓	
Is it serious?		✓
Really?	✓	
What should I do?		✓

2 Really?

3 Doctor, Doctor, everyone keeps ignoring me. NEXT!

Homework

- No specific answers are required for this task, though teachers should check that each joke contains at least one use of a question.

Remember...
We use a **question mark** at the end of a sentence to show that a question has been asked and to invite the reader to think about what the possible answer might be.

Question Marks

Look at these jokes and answer the questions below.

1 Who asks the following questions:

Question	Doctor	Patient
Are you choking?		
Is it serious?		
Really?		
What should I do?		

2 marks

2 Which question is a rhetorical question and does not need an answer?

2 marks

3 Which joke does not include a question?

1 mark

TOP CLASS - Punctuation - Year 4

Question Marks

You are collecting jokes that include questions to help your audience listen out for the punch line. Use different colours to complete each joke and match it with its punch line. Don't forget to add a question mark at the end of each joke.

Question Tag	Joke	Punch Line
What	heavier: a full moon or a crescent moon	Taxi drivers
Where	earns a living driving customers away	A full moon... it's lighter
Why	clothes does a house wear	Because 7, 8, 9
When	ever tried to bend a coin	Tooth hurty
Have you	did the farmer mend his jeans	Address
How	do tadpoles change	With a cabbage patch
Which is	was 6 afraid or 7	In a croak room
Who	did the vampire go to the dentist	Trust me, change is hard

Homework

Collect three jokes that include at least one question in each joke. Practice telling them out loud before writing them down and illustrating them.

Question Marks

You are a comedian. Write down and illustrate a set of jokes you find funny to create a Joke Board that will help you remember them. Do your jokes have a common theme or are they all different? Which ones contain a question to help involve the audience and which do not?

Name: **Date:**

My Joke Board

Exclamation Marks

Think about...
Look at the six signs below.
What type of sign is each one?
Information   Prohibition   Warning   Instruction
Where might you see each sign? Who wrote it? Why?
What might happen if you ignored it?

Guided

Imagine you are training to be a sign writer.

What things would you need to think about when writing a sign? When reading a sign, how important is the setting, purpose and style it has been written in? How does this affect you as a reader? What other text features might a sign writer want to include? Why?

Can you spot any signs in your classroom? What type of signs are they? How have they been written? Why have they been written this way? Once done, answer the questions on page 21.

Independent

Become a sign writer.

On your own, with a partner or in a small group; complete the task sheet provided to you by your teacher on page 22.

Once finished, cut off the homework task to take home with you for further practice.

Extension

Complete the task sheet on page 23.

Once completed, collect examples of signs that use exclamation marks around your local community.

Answers

1 [A] Exclamation Mark, CAPITALS
  [B] <u>Underline</u>
  [C] Exclamation Mark, CAPITALS
  [D] CAPITALS, <u>Underline</u>
  [E] Exclamation Mark, <u>Underline</u>, CAPITALS
  [F] CAPITALS

2 A   B   C   D |E| F

3 (A) BEWARE! FALLING ROCKS
  (C) BEWARE OF DOG — He can reach the gate quicker than you can!

Homework

- No specific answers are required for this task, though teachers should check that each of the examples found has been placed under correct heading.

Remember...
We use an **exclamation mark** to show an intense sense of emotion; especially when following a command or when we are angry. When used at the end of a sentence or after a single word, it implies the writer thinks what they have written is very important.

Exclamation Marks

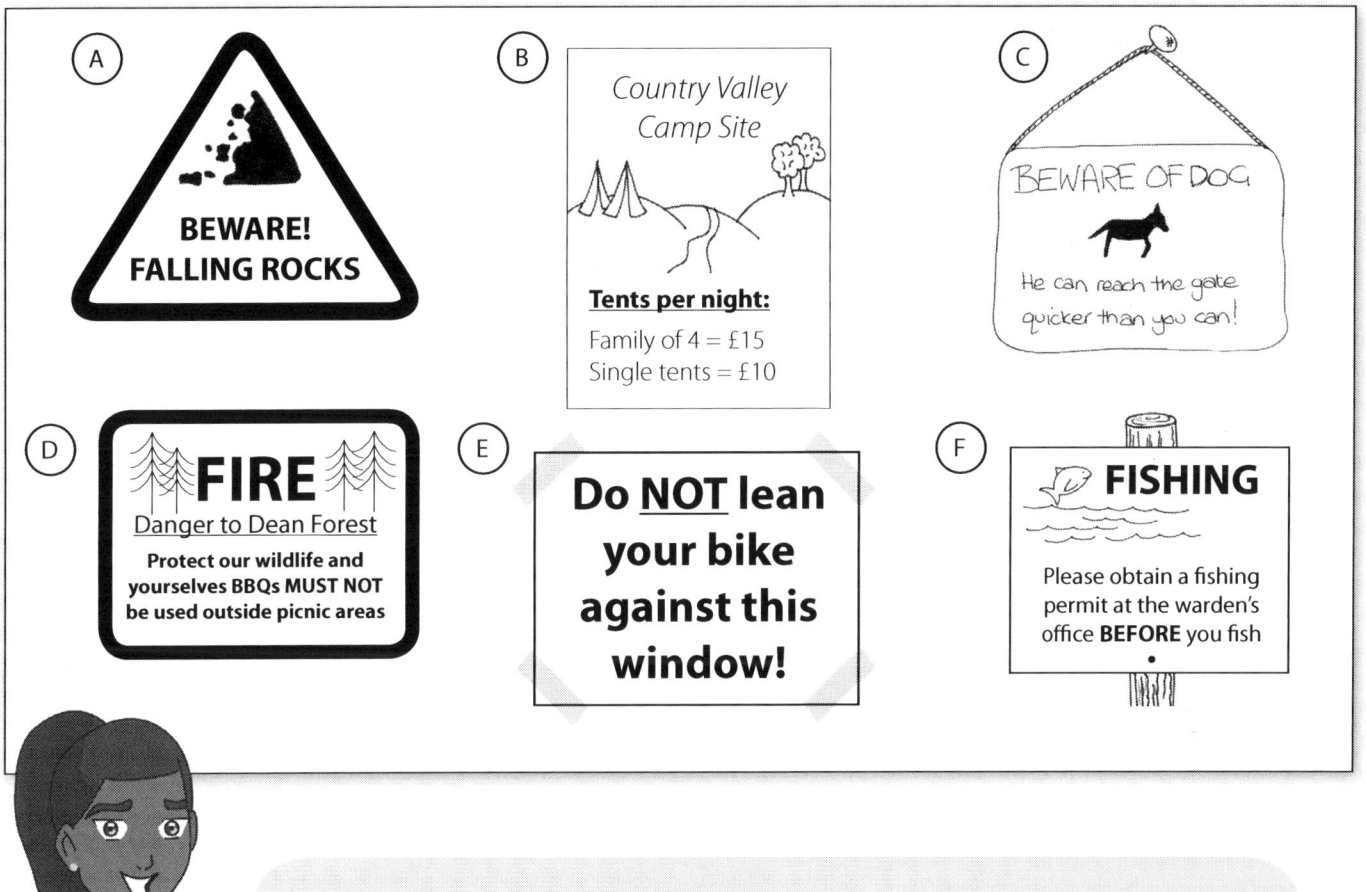

1. How do the signs stress important information?

	STRESS!		
	Exclamation Mark	Underline	CAPITALS
A			
B	✗		
C			
D		✓	
E			✓
F			

3 marks

2. Which sign uses an exclamation mark because they are angry? Tick one box.

A ☐   B ☐   C ☐   D ☐   E ☐   F ☐

1 mark

3. Which two signs use an exclamation mark as a warning?

2 marks

TOP CLASS - Punctuation - Year 4

Exclamation Marks

Design and create different signs for different situations. Where would you see your sign? Why has it been written? Who will read it? What will happen if the sign is ignored? Don't forget to use an exclamation mark when necessary to make your sign stronger.

Sign Here!

	The school cleaner has just mopped the hallway.	
	A park keeper does not want children playing football near the flower beds.	
	A cinema wants to tell its customers about a drink and popcorn deal on offer.	
	A museum wants to direct people to the toilets, including those for the disabled.	
	A pensioner wants to tell his postman to deliver his mail next door.	
	A shopkeeper is angry about the litter dropped outside her shop.	

Homework

Walk around your local community. Photograph or draw different signs you see and put them under the following headings:
Information Prohibition Warning Instruction.
How many of your signs use an exclamation mark?
Why has it been used in these signs and not others?

Exclamation Marks

You are a sign writer! Walk around your school grounds. How many different types of signs you can spot? How have they been written? Why have they been written this way? How has the writer of each sign made important information stand out?

| Name: | Date: |

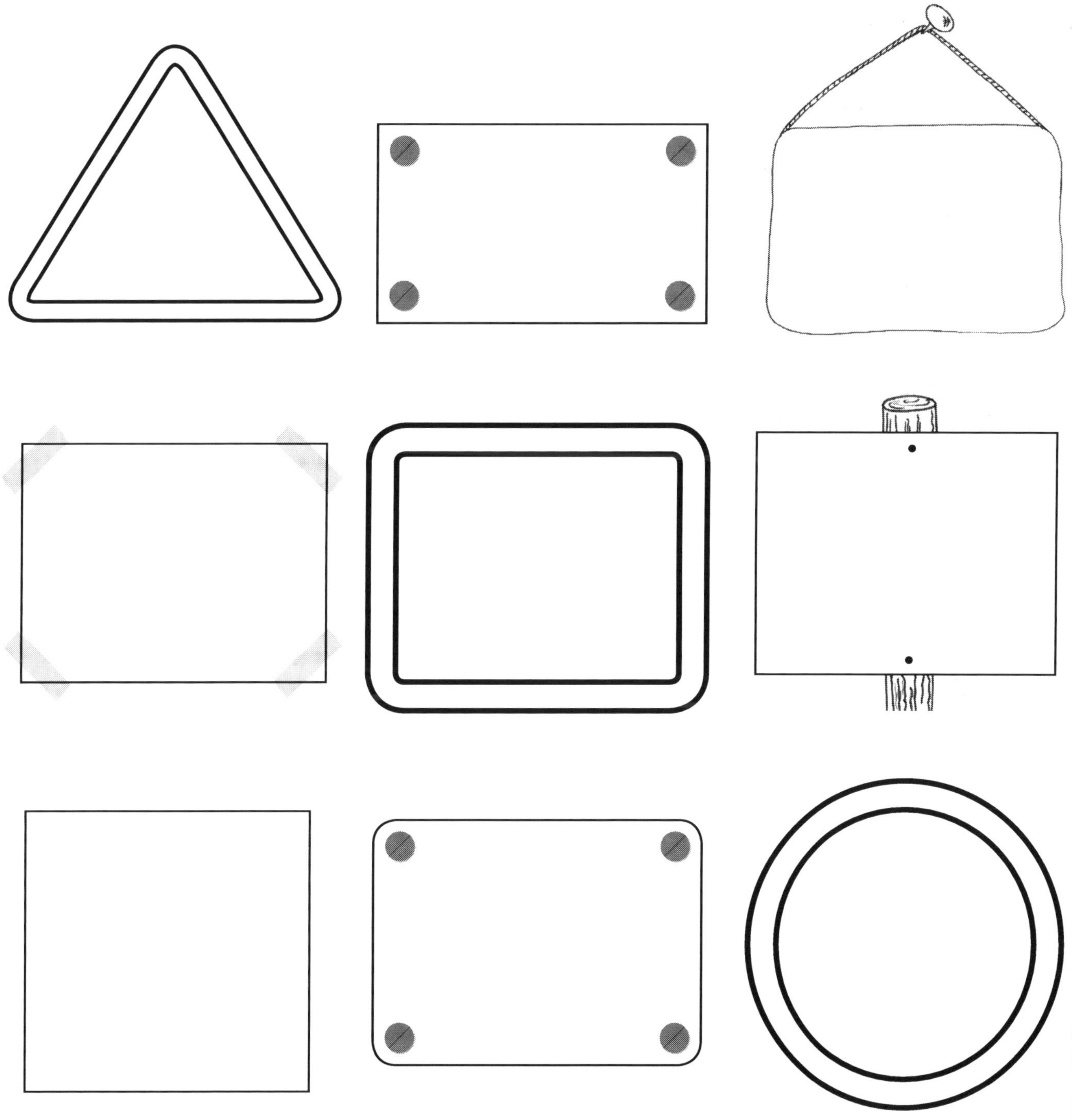

Commas (within lists)

Think about...
Why do people go bird-watching?
What clothes might they wear?
What equipment might they need?
Where might be a good place to go?
What do we call a bird spotter?*

Guided

Imagine you are in a local park bird-watching.

What native birds might you see? How would you identify them? With your teacher, make a list of birds you are likely to see, together with any identifying features they have. Is there anything else you know about the birds you have listed? Share your ideas with your classmates.

Once done, answer the questions on page 25.

Independent

You are asked to help conduct a bird survey.

On your own, with a partner or in a small group; complete the task sheet provided to you by your teacher on page 26.

Once finished, cut off the homework task to take home with you for further practice.

Extension

Take part in a bird watching survey of your own. Complete the task on page 27.

Once completed, think about how you could encourage more birds to visit your school grounds.

Answers

1 1 [2] 3

2 List A: 4 items
List B: 3 items

3 One for sorrow, two for joy, three for a girl, four for a boy, five for silver, six for gold and seven for a secret never to be told.

*A twitcher

Homework

- No specific answers are required for this task, though teachers should check that the lists provided by each learner have included the necessary commas and use of 'and'.

Remember...
We use a **comma** when we are writing a list to show a break between each different item in that list. However, the last two items in the list use 'and' between them instead of a comma.

24   TOP CLASS - Punctuation - Year 4

Commas (within lists)

Of all the birds that grace our skies, it is the magpie that we most associate with bad luck. Throughout Britain it is considered unlucky to see a lone magpie and in many parts of the UK people will salute a single magpie whilst saying "Good morning Mr Magpie. How is your lady wife today?"

By acknowledging the magpie in this way you are showing him proper respect, in the hope that he will not pass on bad fortune to you. And by referring to the magpie's wife, you are implying that there are two magpies, which brings joy rather than sorrow according to the popular children's rhyme:

> One for sorrow, two for joy, three for a girl and four for a boy.
> Five for silver, six for gold and seven for a secret never to be told.

Look at this superstition and answer the questions below.

1 How many lists are in the children's rhyme?

  1   2   3

1 mark

2 How many items are listed in each list?

List A:	List B:

2 marks

3 Rewrite this children's rhyme to make it into a single list.

_____

_____

_____

3 marks

Commas (within lists)

Look at your notes. Group the birds together according to where you spotted them. Put each list in alphabetical order. Don't forget to use a comma between each bird and remember to use 'and' between the last two.

My Bird Survey:

Sparrow (bush) - 4
Pigeon (playground) - 6
Blackbird (bush) - 1
Thrush (bush) - 2
Starling (woodland) - 5
Blue tit (woodland) - 4
Heron (lake) - 2
Greenfinch (woodland) - 3
Robin (woodland) - 2
Kestrel (woodland) - 1
Swan (lake) - 6
Swallow (lake) - 4
Coot (lake) - 4
Dove (playground) - 2
Woodpecker (woodland) - 1
Canada goose (lake) - 8
Mallard (lake) - 5
Magpie (playground) - 1

Bush

Woodland

Lake

Playground

Homework

Write a list for each of the following:
- Five sea birds
- Three birds that are flightless
- Four different types of owls
- Six birds that have black feathers

Commas (within lists)

Visit a local park and conduct your own bird survey.
What equipment will you need?
How will you log what birds you see and where you spot them?
How will you present your results?

Name: **Date:**

Trees

Sky

I will need:

Bushes

By Water

To take part in *The Big Schools' Bird Watch* visit: **www.rspb.org**

Commas (within clauses)

Think about...
Look at this sentence from a nursery rhyme:
Mary had a little lamb its fleece was white as snow.
Where should the comma go? Why?
Colour the two parts: Mary (blue), the lamb (red).

Guided

You are reading a friend's poem about the Fun Fair they visited in the summer holidays.

What things might your friend have included in their poem? Make a list with a partner. Draw and label your ideas.

Once done, share your ideas with your teacher. Then answer the questions on page 29.

Independent

Your friend has typed out a poem to read to his class.

On your own, with a partner or in a small group; complete the task sheet provided to you by your teacher on page 30.

Once finished, cut off the homework task to take home with you for further practice.

Extension

Write your own poem about a Fun Fair. Complete the task sheet on page 31.

Once completed, put your poem in a class anthology of poems.

Answers

1 Lights and laughter fill the air,
Applause and music everywhere.

2 Verse 8

3 Because

Homework

- No specific answers are required for this task, though teachers should check that the general ideas collected by each learner have kept to the theme of the proposed poem.

Remember...
We use a **comma** to break up a long sentence to make it easier to read. In poems with rhyming couplets, we often put a comma at the end of the first line to signal the end of the first clause.

Commas (within clauses)

FUN FAIR

Roll up, roll up, come one and all,
The fair's in town, let's have a ball.

Tightrope walkers, fortune tellers
Bearded ladies (or are they fellas?)

Dodgem cars that bump and bash,
Like charging rhinos they do CRASH!

Clowns in unicycle races,
Water pistols, made-up faces.

Down the helter-skelter slide,
Round and round, mouths opened wide.

Fire eaters, acrobats,
Lion tamers, tall black hats.

Hoopla, loopla, bag a fish,
Cross your fingers, make a wish.

Finally, the Grand Parade,
Candy floss and lemonade.

Roll up, roll up, come everyone,
The fair's in town, we'll have such fun.

Look at this poem and answer the questions below.

1 Split this new verse into two clauses using a comma.
Colour the first clause yellow and the second clause pink.

Lights and laughter fill the air

Applause and music everywhere.

2 marks

2 In which verse do you see a comma used after a time connective?

Verse 1 ☐	Verse 2 ☐	Verse 3 ☐
Verse 4 ☐	Verse 5 ☐	Verse 6 ☐
Verse 7 ☐	Verse 8 ☐	Verse 9 ☐

1 mark

3 Which of these words would not be followed by a comma?

Firstly   **Lastly**   **However**   **Because**

1 mark

Commas (within clauses)

A computer virus has attacked your friend's computer. It has deleted the commas and mixed up the verses to his favourite poem. Help your friend rewrite the poem in the correct order. Don't forget to use a comma to end the first line of each verse to signal where the first clause ends.

A poem:

Dull November brings the blast
Then the leaves go whirling past.

April brings the primrose sweet
Scatters daisies at our feet.

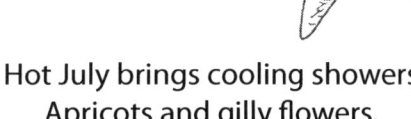

Hot July brings cooling showers
Apricots and gilly flowers.

March brings breezes sharp and shrill
Shakes the dancing daffodil.

Warm September brings the fruit
Sportsmen then begin to shoot.

Brown October brings the pheasant
Then to gather nuts is pleasant.

January brings the snow
Makes our feet and fingers glow.

August brings the sheaves of corn
Then the harvest home is borne.

May brings flocks of pretty lambs
Skipping by their fleecy dams.

Chill December brings the sleet
Blazing fire and Christmas treat.

June brings tulips, lillies, roses
Fills the children's hands with posies.

February brings the rain
Thaws the frozen lake again.

Homework

Collect some ideas for a poem about a summer fair that visits where you live.
What do you see there? Who do you meet?
Do you go on any rides? How do you feel?
What sounds do you hear? What smells do you smell?

Commas (within clauses)

After you have collected some ideas for your Fun Fair poem, begin to put them together to write a first draft. Put each rhyming couplet you think of on two separate lines to form each verse. What do you see? Who do you visit? What rides do you go on? Do you win anything? What can you hear? What can you smell?

Name: **Date:**

FUN FAIR

Roll up, roll up, come one and all,
The fair's in town, let's have a ball.

Inverted Commas

Think about...
What is the difference between a dream and a nightmare? What might happen in a dream that might not happen in real life?
Who might speak in a dream? How would you show this if you were writing your dream down?

Guided

Think about a vivid dream you have had in the past.

Where was your dream set? What happened in your dream? Who were the main characters? What did they say? How did they speak? How did your dream end?

Once done, find a talk partner and tell them about your dream. Compare your dream to the one your talk partner had.

Then, answer the questions on page 33.

Independent

You are reading the end to chapter 1 of a children's book called 'Dreamscape'.

On your own, with a partner or in a small group; complete the task sheet provided to you by your teacher on page 34.

Once finished, cut off the homework task to take home with you for further practice.

Extension

Write about a dream you have had. Complete the task sheet on page 35.

Once completed, why not keep a dream diary next to your bed so that you can jot down any fantastical dreams you have?

Answers

1 Red
Blue
Blue
Yellow
Yellow
Blue
Blue

2 'Did you enjoy your dream, Alice?' asked her sister.

3 'Allow for a child's own words,' screamed the Queen.

Homework

- No specific answers are required for this task, though teachers should check that inverted commas have been used correctly when writing the dialogue between the Goblin King and the main character.

Remember...
We use **inverted commas** (or **speech marks**) to show which words are being spoken by a character in a story.

Inverted Commas

Alice in Wonderland

`Off with her head!' the Queen shouted at the top of her voice. Nobody moved.

`Who cares for you?' said Alice, (she had grown to her full size by this time) `You're nothing but a pack of cards!'

At this the whole pack rose up into the air, and came flying down upon her: she gave a little scream, half of fright and half of anger, and tried to beat them off, and found herself lying on the bank, with her head in the lap of her sister, who was gently brushing away some dead leaves that had fluttered down from the trees upon her face.

`Wake up, Alice dear!' said her sister; `Why, what a long sleep you've had!'

`Oh, I've had such a curious dream!' said Alice, and she told her sister, as well as she could remember them, all these strange Adventures of hers that you have just been reading about; and when she had finished, her sister kissed her, and said, `It WAS a curious dream, dear, certainly: but now run in to your tea; it's getting late.' So Alice got up and ran off, thinking while she ran, as well she might, what a wonderful dream it had been.

Look at this classic and answer the questions below.

1 Colour the speech for each of the three characters:

Red = The Queen of Hearts   Blue = Alice   Green = Alice's sister

3 marks

2 Where should the speech marks go in the sentence below?

Did you enjoy your dream, Alice? asked her sister.

2 marks

3 What do you think the Queen would have said when Alice woke up?

_____ screamed the Queen.   *2 marks*

TOP CLASS - Punctuation - Year 4

Inverted Commas

You are reading the end of Chapter 1 of 'Dreamscape'. However, you notice that the publishers have made a printing error and forgotten to put speech marks around the spoken text. You decide to show them their mistake. Find the parts of the text that are spoken and put in the necessary speech marks.

Key: *Goblin King = Green   Goblins = Red   Dreamer = Yellow   Mum = Blue*

Dreamscape

I had little time to act, for I knew the Goblin King and his warriors were not far behind.

I could hear his shrill voice cackle somewhere in the shadowy distance.

I want the human alive I tell you...alive!

I leapt on to the back of Crystal, my trusted unicorn, and whispered in her ear.

In the name of all that is good, hurry!

The grunts and the groans of the goblins drew ever nearer, the shrieks and the screams surrounding us both on the ground and in the tree tops above us.

Catch the human, catch the human, they chanted.

Suddenly, Crystal stopped, uncertain as to which path to take.

What's up? Why have you stopped?

Seconds later, I had my answer...

Time to get up, mum said. You don't want to be late on your first day back, do you?

And with that, I turned off my alarm clock and got out of bed.

Homework

What might have happened if mum hadn't broken the dreamer's dream? Rewrite the ending to Chapter 1 of 'Dreamscape'. Include dialogue between the Goblin King and the main character.

Inverted Commas

Write an entry in your Dream Journal.
Where was your dream set?
What happened in your dream?
Who were the main characters? What did they say?
How did they speak?
How did your dream end?

Name: | **Date:**

The Dream

My eyes closed. I knew I would soon be transported there once again...Dreamland!

It was such a magical place, where time stood still and anything could happen. But this night was different. The wonderful world I knew so well was about to change forever.

Apostrophes (for omission)

Think about...
Why do people read and write poetry?
What kind of poems do you like best? Why?
What is a shape poem?
Do you think a shape poem will be formal or informal? Why?

Guided

Imagine you are reading a shape poem to help inspire your own work.

What is this shape poem about? Why do you think it is shaped like this? Why is the first word written in this way? Who do you think the writer's intended audience is? Why? Did you like the poem?

Once discussed, answer the questions on page 37.

Independent

Read part of an interview with children's poet Ian Bland, author of My Rocket Ship.

On your own, with a partner or in a small group; complete the task sheet provided to you by your teacher on page 38.

Once finished, cut off the homework task to take home with you for further practice.

Extension

Use Ian's poem to inspire you to write your own shape poem about something you make out of junk. Complete the task sheet on page 39.

Once completed, send your shape poems to Ian himself via his website or publish your work in a class anthology.

Answers

1
- It's = Uses an apostrophe to contract two words (it is). It is more informal.
- Its = This is a single word in its own right so does not need an apostrophe.

2

Negative Form	
Formal	Informal
did not	didn't
could not	couldn't
should not	shouldn't
would not	wouldn't
will not	won't*
do not	don't

*irregular

3 Formal: It is not

Informal: it's not or it isn't

Homework

- No specific answers are required for this task, though teachers should check that the shape poem provided by each learner includes at least one correct use of an apostrophe being used for informal contraction.

Remember...
We use an **apostrophe** to join two words together. This is informal so we usually use this when writing or speaking to friends or family or when the situation is relaxed and friendly too.

Apostrophes (for omission)

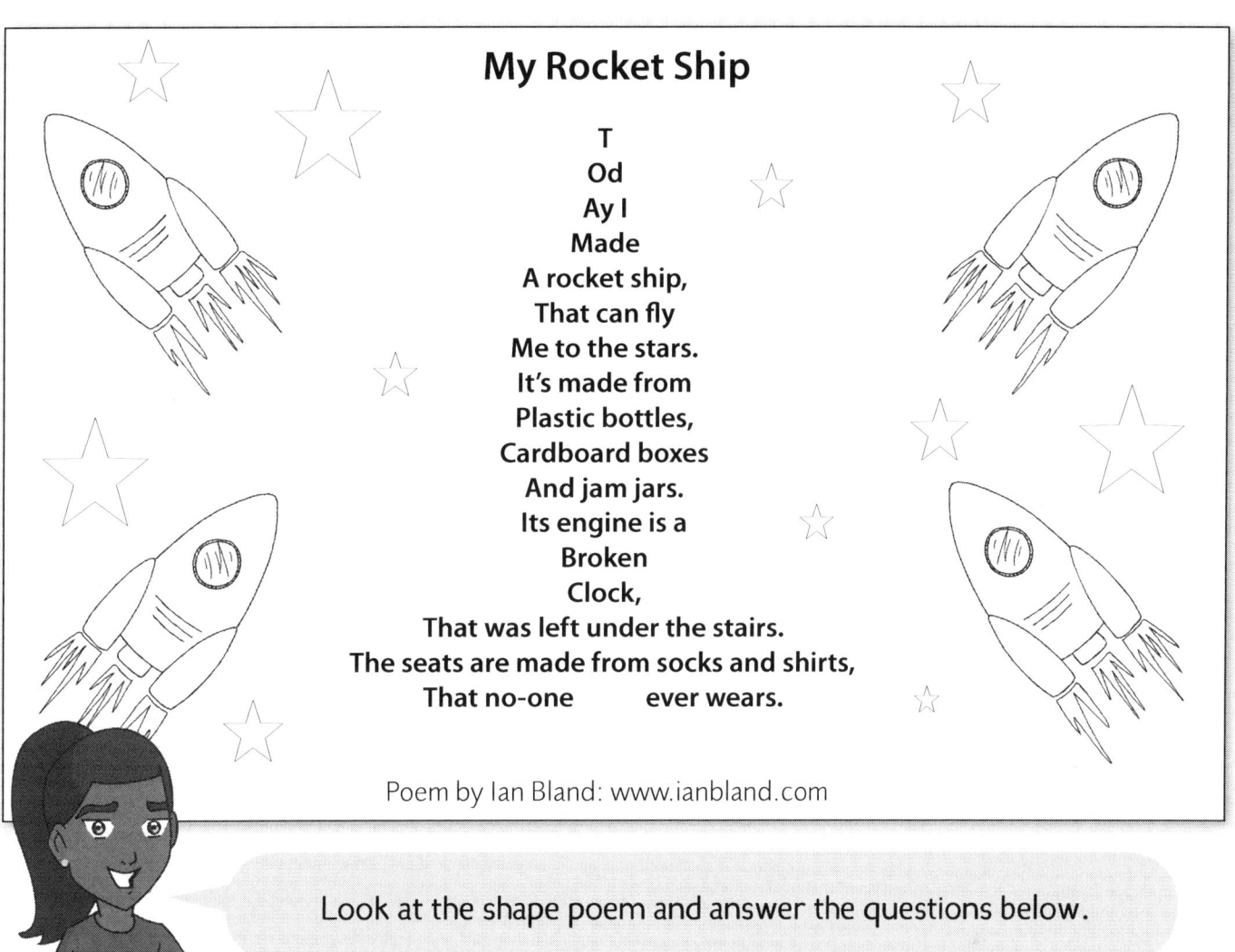

My Rocket Ship

T
Od
Ay I
Made
A rocket ship,
That can fly
Me to the stars.
It's made from
Plastic bottles,
Cardboard boxes
And jam jars.
Its engine is a
Broken
Clock,
That was left under the stairs.
The seats are made from socks and shirts,
That no-one   ever wears.

Poem by Ian Bland: www.ianbland.com

Look at the shape poem and answer the questions below.

1 Find the following two words. Why are they different? What do they mean?

It's _____

Its _____

4 marks

2 Fill in the table below. Put a star next to the irregular spelling.

Negative Form	
Formal	Informal
did not	
	couldn't
should not	
	wouldn't
will not	
	don't

3 marks

3 Change it's into the negative form.

Formal:	Informal:

3 marks

TOP CLASS - Punctuation - Year 4

Apostrophes (for omission)

Read part of an interview with Ian Bland. It was a very relaxed interview. How can you tell?
Highlight the evidence for this.
There are ten different contractions for you to spot.

An Informal Chat:

So tell us Ian, why did you become a poet?

I've always been fascinated by words and the power they possess. As a child, I enjoyed stories and songs but the genre that fascinated me the most was poetry. Given the slightest opportunity I'd be scribbling down ideas and begging the nearest person around me to listen to my latest work!

When I was training to be a teacher, part of my degree was about creative writing so I began to get serious about poetry at university. However, it wasn't until I became a teacher that I really decided to become a children's poet.

My favourite lesson to teach was Literacy and I naturally gravitated towards poetry. If I couldn't find a suitable poem for a lesson, I'd just write it myself. Eventually, I managed to get some work published, though this didn't happen over night. Not getting published straight away can knock your confidence but I know I'm a stronger poet for it. In fact, if there's any advice I could offer any budding young poets it'd be this: enjoy the process of writing and performing your poetry. Read lots of poems for inspiration and, whatever you do, don't give up on your dream of seeing your work in print.

Now I travel the UK and Europe performing and leading poetry workshops for children and training teachers; it's great fun. I feel like I've got the best job in the world!

Homework

Go on an apostrophe hunt!
Find ten examples of when two words have been joined together using an apostrophe.
Make a list of where you found each example and think about how you would write it formally as two words.

Apostrophes (for omission)

Use Ian's poem to inspire you to draft your own shape poem made out of junk.
What will you make? What junk will you use?
What shape will it be?
How will you present your work to others?

Name:	Date:

Last night I made _____

That can _____

It's made from _____

Its_____

_____

_____

Its_____

_____

_____

Its_____

_____

_____

Its_____

_____

_____

Apostrophes (for possession)

Think about...
Make a list of five things that you own.
Make a list of things your classmates own.
Compare your two lists. How are they similar?
How are they different?
How have you used an apostrophe in each list?

Guided

Imagine you are lost and stumble across a castle in the dead of night.

As a group, draw your setting and add notes to your sketch. What might you see? What might you hear? What might the weather be like? Who might live in the castle? What might they be doing? What genre of story do you think you are about to read? Why do you think this?

Once done, answer the questions on page 41.

Independent

You enter the castle to shelter from the storm.

On your own, with a partner or in a small group; complete the task sheet provided to you by your teacher on page 42.

Once finished, cut off the homework task to take home with you for further practice.

Extension

Write the next part of the story. Complete the task sheet on page 43.

Once completed, publish your chapter on the computer!

Answers

1 Dr Frankenstein

2 The night

3 (beyond the forest's shadows)

Homework

- Mary Shelly's Frankenstein (1818)
- Bram Stoker's Dracula (1897)
- Robert Louis Stevenson's Dr Jekyll and Mr Hyde (1886)
- Gaston Leroux's Phantom of the Opera (1909)*

*Translated from the original French into English in 1911

Remember...
We add an **apostrophe** (**'s**) to show possession. If a person's name already ends with 's' then we only need to add the apostrophe on its own.

Apostrophes (for possession)

HE'S ALIVE!

A crash of thunder rumbles and tumbles in the heavens above as a lightning bolt licks the night's sky and unmasks the eerie shape silhouetted before me.

Driving rain beats down and the wind snakes its way around the craggy rocks upon which Dr Frankenstein's castle sits; a screaming banshee of terror and excitement.

And if you look closely enough (beyond the shadows of the forest) there, in an upper room, is a lonely window bathed in a strange flickering light...a blinking eye looking down on the world below.

And if you listen closer still, through the thunder and the rain, through the wind and the beating of your heart, you will make out the cries of a mad man...

'He's alive. He's alive! HE'S ALIVE!'

Look at this extract from a horror story and answer the questions below.

1 Who owns the castle?

_____ *1 mark*

2 Who does the sky belong to?

_____ *2 marks*

3 Rewrite the words in brackets to show that the shadows belong to the forest.

_____ *2 marks*

TOP CLASS - Punctuation - Year 4

Apostrophes (for possession)

You enter Dr Frankenstein's castle to shelter from the storm. You look around and see many things that belong to various monsters. What objects do you see? Who do they belong to? Where did you find them? Use an apostrophe to show who owns which object and where you found it.

What did you see?

1. I saw Vinny the vampire's false teeth in the toilet.
2.
3.
4.
5.
6.
7.
8.

Vinny the vampire ✓   Gary the ghost

Wendy the witch   Rob the robot

false teeth ✓

ball & chain   broom stick

oil can   dungeon   library

cellar   hallway   spanner

attic   kitchen

laboratory   toilet ✓

handkerchief   lab coat

bandages

Frankenstein   Bob the blob

Maggie the mummy   Dr Frankenstein

Homework

Find out who created the following monsters and when.
- Frankenstein
- Dracula
- Dr Jekyll and Mr Hyde
- The Phantom of the Opera

Apostrophes (for possession)

Write the conclusion to this story. Do you spot anything that could aid your escape? What is it? Who does it belong to? In what location did you find it? Do you hear any eerie sounds? Who do they belong to? Do you eventually escape or not?

Name:　　　　　　　　　　　　　　　**Date:**

THE ESCAPE

TOP CLASS - Punctuation - Year 4

Brackets

Think about...
How heavy were you when you were born?
How tall are you now?
How would you write down this information?
Would you use metric or imperial? Why?
Why might it be important to both?

Guided

You have taken a wildlife book out of your school library.

What information might we expect to read about this animal on this page? Make a list with a partner. Snowball this list with another pair and compare your list of ideas. Snowball again with another group one last time.

Once done, feedback your ideas to your teacher. Then answer the questions on page 45.

Independent

You are trying to look up some fascinating facts about speed.

On your own, with a partner or in a small group; complete the task sheet provided to you by your teacher on page 46.

Once finished, cut off the homework task to take home with you for further practice.

Extension

It's all about you! Complete the task sheet on page 47.

Once completed, compare your measurements with your classmates. Work out the average height for your class. Are you above or below average? Who is closest to the average? Display your results in a class graph using both metric and imperial units.

Answers

1

Metric	Imperial
130 kg	290 lb
375 kg	826 lb
180 kg	400 lb
8 kilometres	5 miles
80 kph	50 mph

2 Because his audience are younger and used to metric measures.

3 We find out what a female lion is called (a lioness).

Homework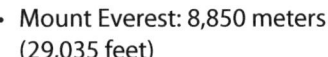

- Mount Everest: 8,850 meters (29,035 feet)
- The Blue Whale: 170 tonnes (26,770 stones)
- The stapes: 0.25 centimetres (0.1 inches)
- The Great Wall of China: 3460 kilometres (2150 miles)

Remember...
Writers use **brackets** when we want to give the reader extra information in a sentence but also want to keep it separate. However, sometimes this is also because the writer wants to include other readers that will understand the information inside the brackets better.

Brackets

Long Live the King!

 When lions breed with tigers the resulting hybrids are known as *ligers* and *tigons*.

 Lions can reach speeds of up to 80 kph (50 mph) but only in short bursts because of a lack of stamina.

 The heaviest lion on record weighed an amazing 375 kg (826 lb).

 Lions in the wild live for around 12 years, resting each day for up to 20 hours.

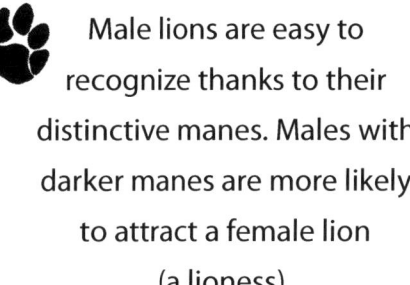 Male lions are easy to recognize thanks to their distinctive manes. Males with darker manes are more likely to attract a female lion (a lioness).

 The average male lion weighs around 180 kg (400 lb) while the average female lion weighs around 130 kg (290 lb).

 The roar of a lion can be heard from 8 kilometers (5 miles) away.

Look at the Fact File and answer the questions below.

1 Fill in the conversion table below.

Metric	Imperial
130 kg	
375 kg	
	400 lb
	5 miles
80 kph	

2 marks

2 Why do you think the writer puts the imperial measure in brackets and not the metric?

_____

2 marks

3 How else does the writer use brackets to give us new information?

_____

2 marks

Brackets

You are doing some research on how fast different things can travel. Look on the Internet and see if you can find out how fast the following things can go. Then write this information down in a sentence. Don't forget to put the imperial measure of speed in brackets.

How Fast...

...can a human run?		A human runs at 9.6 kph (6 mph).
...can a cheetah run?		
...can an ostrich run?		
...can a peregrine falcon fly?		
...can a shark swim?		
...can a plane travel?		

Homework

Find out the following record holders:
- The tallest mountain in the world
- The heaviest creature on the planet
- The smallest bone in the human body
- The longest wall ever built

Brackets

You want to present some information about yourself and want as many people to read it as possible. For this reason, you decide to write your facts in both metric and imperial. With a friend collect your data. What instruments will you use? What do you estimate your measure will be? What is it in reality?

Name: | **Date:**

How heavy were you when you were born?

What is your present weight?

How tall are you now?

Me, Myself & I

How long is your hair?

How big are your feet?

TOP CLASS - Punctuation - Year 4

Ellipses

Think about...
Look at this sentence:
She stared at the letter box...nothing!
What do you think she was waiting for? Did she wait for a long or short time? How did she feel when nothing arrived? What might this suggest?

Guided

Imagine you are a tooth fairy working for the Tooth Express Delivery Service.

What would your job be? How much would you leave for each tooth? Where would you leave it? What might happen when you got back from work and saw your boss?

Once done, practice acting out this comedy sketch with a partner.* Then answer the questions on page 49.

You may want to remind them to pause for a lengthy time when they see the ellipses and discuss how this will add to the comedy of anticipating the punch line.

Independent

You are editing a comedy sketch with your co-writer.

On your own, with a partner or in a small group; complete the task sheet provided to you by your teacher on page 50.

Once finished, cut off the homework task to take home with you for further practice.

Extension

Write a comedy sketch for you and a friend. Complete the task sheet on page 51.

Once done, learn your script and act it out!

Answers

1 Yes, Yes

2 Choose from either of the following:
- Ten pence was the rate when I was a youngster...TEN PENCE!

or
- Stick it on the window sill and cover it in fairy dust for all I care...JUST GET MY POUND BACK!

3 He sold the cow for a packet of magic beans...MAGIC BEANS!

Homework

- No specific answers are required for this task, though teachers should check that the joke provided by each learner has included an ellipses being used to help deliver a punch line. Get learners to deliver their jokes to the class to see the ellipses in action!

Remember...
We use **ellipses** (...) when we want to show the passage of time for dramatic or comical effect. It makes the reader wait for what comes next. This raises the tension in a dramatic scene or helps deliver the punch line in a comedy sketch.

Ellipses

Pull the Other One

A pound? A POUND!

For a tooth? FOR A TOOTH!

That's £20 per child! I'm not made of money you know.
We're supposed to give them silver...SILVER. Not gold! Could you imagine if we had to play this game with Granny Smith over there with her new set of pearly whites? That would have cost me another £32...I'd be bankrupt! Ten pence was the rate when I was a youngster...TEN PENCE! No, it simply won't do. Take it back!

Take it back? And where exactly do you want me to stick it when I get there, under her pillow...or back in her mouth?

Stick it on the window sill and cover it with fairy dust for all I care...JUST GET MY POUND BACK!

Look at the comedy sketch and answer the questions below.

1 Look at the first ellipsis. How is it used here?

To show time passing.	Yes / No
To infer anger is building up.	Yes / No

2 marks

2 Write out another example from the text where this is the case.

_____

_____

2 marks

3 Rewrite the sentence below in the same style as the writer. Use an ellipsis.

He sold the cow for a packet of magic beans.

_____

3 marks

TOP CLASS - Punctuation - Year 4

Ellipses

You are asked to edit the first draft of a comedy sketch. How might you make this funnier? Don't forget to use ellipses to lead your audience to the punch line and make them laugh. In small groups, act it out to see if you were right.

A Fishy Tale:

Shop Keeper: [*Holds up the sign to his customers: 'Fresh Fish Sold Here!'*] Hey, do you like my new sign?

Customer 1: [*Shaking head*] 'Fresh'. You don't need the word 'Fresh'. Of course it's fresh. What else would it be? Rotten!

[*He tears off the word 'Fresh' and walks out of the shop*].

Customer 2: [*Sighing*] 'Fish'. You don't need the word 'Fish'. You're a fish shop; what else would you be selling? Lawn mowers!

[*He tears off the word 'Fish' and walks out of the shop*].

Customer 3: [*Tutting and wagging finger*] 'Sold'. You don't need the word 'Sold'. You're a shop, what else would you do? Give it away!

[*He tears off the word 'Sold' and walks out of the shop*].

Customer 4: [*Stroking chin*] 'Here'. You don't need the word 'Here'. Everyone knows it's 'Here'. Where else would you be selling it? Timbuktu!

[*He tears off the word 'Here' and walks out of the shop*].

New customer: [*Walking in to the shop*] Good morning, do you sell lawn mowers?

Shop Keeper: No. I only sell fresh fish here.

New customer: Oh, I see. Pity, I'd put a sign in the window if I were you!

Homework

Find a joke that uses ellipses to help deliver the punch line (adapt your favourite joke if you want to). Write out your joke and practice delivering it out loud to get ready for a class comedy club your teacher will set up.

Ellipses

You are a comedy writer writing the second part to the Pull the Other One sketch.
What happens when the tooth fairy takes the tooth back?
Is the child awake?
Does the child want to give their pound back?
What happens next?

Name:	Date:

Pull the Other One

Part II

Scene: *The tooth fairy is stood at the end of the bed, scratching their head, tooth in hand.*

Tooth Fairy:

Child:

Tooth Fairy:

Child:

Tooth Fairy:

Child:

Tooth Fairy:

Child:

Tooth Fairy:

Child:

Colons

Think about...
How many different superheroes can you think of in sixty seconds?
Compare Superman and Spiderman.
How are they similar? How are they different?
How will you use a colon in each of your lists?

Guided

Imagine you are listening to a friend talking about their nan.

What do you expect they will talk about? Why do you think this? Discuss your ideas as a class with your teacher. Listen to what is actually talked about. How does it compare the ideas you and your classmates came up with beforehand?

Once discussed, answer the questions on page 53.

Independent

You have just discovered that your grandma is a secret superhero!

On your own, with a partner or in a small group; complete the task sheet provided to you by your teacher on page 54.

Once finished, cut off the homework task to take home with you for further practice.

Extension

Create a superhero for a new comic coming out soon. Complete the task sheet on page 55.

Once completed, plan a comic strip story of how your superhero got their super powers. Use lots of different punctuation in their speech and thought bubbles.

Answers

1 Because the writer wants to write a list of what nans are supposed to be like.
(Allow variations on this idea)

2 My granddad loved sport: cricket, football and tennis.

3 Granny Jones liked to wear lots of things: a pearl necklace, pink slippers, false teeth but not her hearing aid.

Homework

- Venom is an enemy of Spiderman. He is first seen in 'The Alien Costume' storyline of The Amazing Spider-Man (Marvel Comics) published in May 1984.
- General Zod is one of Superman's greatest enemies. He is first seen in Adventure Comics (DC Comics) published in April 1961.
- The Joker is the arch enemy of Batman. His character is introduced in the first ever Batman comic (DC Comics) published April 25th, 1940.

Remember...
We use a **colon** to show that we are going to write a list.

Colons

My Nan

Nan, grandma, granny...whatever you call her (and let's face it, aged 187 she's as old as the hills and as deaf as a doorpost so she probably won't hear you anyway) our nans are supposed to be the same the world over: good cooks, great knitters and galactic gossipers.

But not my nan. Oh no!

Gave everything the taste of charred toast, the only thing she knitted was her brow and spoke only to tell you to 'stop mumbling child and speak up'. In fact, you wouldn't hear a peep from her until it was time to say good bye, her words sealed with a gummy kiss.

My nan is no longer with us; passed away years ago. But when I see her in photographs or listen out for her in the corners of my memory, a smile always creeps upon my face and a giggle, wriggles somewhere deep inside me.

Why? Because she was my nan: not yours, not Billy Grimshaw's from down the road, not Jennifer Spittlethwaite's or her twin brother Charles'. No, she was my nan and I loved her very much.

Look at this anecdote and answer the questions below.

1 Why does the writer use a colon in the first paragraph?

1 mark

2 Which sentence is punctuated correctly? Tick one box.

My granddad loved sport cricket, football and tennis. ☐

My granddad loved: sport cricket, football and tennis. ☐

My granddad loved sport: cricket, football and tennis. ☐

My granddad: loved sport cricket, football and tennis. ☐

1 mark

3 Where should the colon go in the following sentence?

Granny Jones liked to wear lots of things a pearl necklace, pink slippers and false teeth but not her hearing aid.

2 marks

TOP CLASS - Punctuation - Year 4

Colons

You have just discovered that your gran is a secret superhero! Make a list of all her superhero qualities under each of the headings. Don't forget to use a colon before you start each list.

My Gran:

Supergran

Appearance	Costume	Super Powers

Enemies	Battle Scenes

- What did she look like?
- What was her costume like?
- What super powers did she have?
- Who did she do battle with?
- Where did these battles take place?

Homework

Which superhero is associated with the following villains?
- Venom
- General Zod
- The Joker

In which comic did they first appear?

Colons

Create your own superhero for a new comic that is coming out soon! What do they look like?
What powers do they have?
How did they get their powers?
Who do they fight with and where?

Name: **Date:**

WOW!   AMAZING!

_____

| Appearance | Costume | Super Powers |

| Enemies | Battle Scenes |

_____
_____
_____
_____
_____

TOP CLASS - Punctuation - Year 4

Semi-colons

Think about...
Put the following marks in order of pause length (. , ;) Which mark goes in the middle? Why? Where does it go in this sentence: Claire was born at 16:24 Simon was close behind at 16:32. Why do you think it goes here?

Guided

You are a Year 4 class teacher who is writing an end of year school report.

Who are you going to write about: the teacher's pet or the class joker? What will you need to write about? What do you want to tell their parents? What do you want to tell your pupil themselves? How will you tell the truth without upsetting them if you have chosen the class joker? List your ideas with your teacher.

Once done, answer the questions on page 57.

Independent

You are a teacher setting your class some punctuation homework.

On your own, with a partner or in a small group; complete the task sheet provided to you by your teacher on page 58.

Once finished, cut off the homework task to take home with you for further practice.

Extension

Write a school report about a child you have been teaching in Year 4. Complete the task sheet on page 59.

Once done, look back at your own school report from last year. How does it compare?

Answers

1 It has been a pleasure teaching Sally so it is with great sadness that I will see her leave.

His uniform must be pristine although it is a pity he no longer needs it.

2 No one was seriously hurt in the accident; one man suffered a broken finger.

3 Americans call it soccer; we call it football.

Homework

- No specific answers are required for this task, though teachers should check that the sentence provided by each learner has included a semi-colon. Where possible, this sentence should also have been rewritten so that the two clauses have swapped position but the sentence as a whole still makes sense.

Remember...
It is very rare that we use a **semi-colon**. It is half way between a comma and a full stop and acts as a strong pause that links two parts of a sentence.

Semi-colons

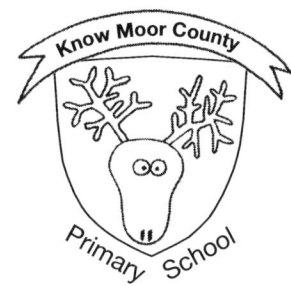

General: It has been a pleasure teaching Sally; it is with great sadness that I will see her leave.

She has been a ray of sunshine throughout the year; I am sure her positive attitude towards her work and others will continue to shine through into her new school.

Good luck Sally, you have a bright future ahead of you!

Teacher: *Mr Page*

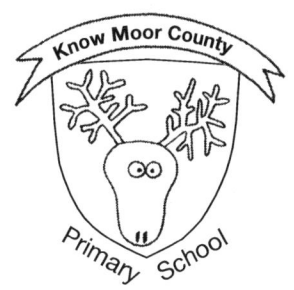

General: Like the invisible man, I have not seen much of Harry this year. If lack of attendance was an Olympic sport, he would be a gold medallist!

His uniform must be pristine; it is a pity he no longer needs it.

You have the potential to do great things Harry; you will find it difficult to achieve anything whilst in bed.

Teacher: *Mr Page*

Look at these school reports and answer the questions below.

1 Draw a line to match each sentence with the best connective to replace the semi-colon.

| although |
| because |
| so |

It has been a pleasure teaching Sally; it is with great sadness that I will see her leave.

His uniform must be pristine; it is a pity he no longer needs it.

2 marks

2 Put a semi-colon in the sentence below. Colour each clause in a different colour.

No one was seriously hurt in the accident one man suffered a broken finger.

2 marks

3 Put a semi-colon in the sentence below. Colour each clause in a different colour.

Americans call it soccer we call it football.

2 marks

TOP CLASS - Punctuation - Year 4

Semi-colons

You are a Year 4 class teacher and want to set your class some punctuation homework. You want to check if you can match the two clauses to make a sentence. Don't forget to use a semi-colon to show a big pause.

Punctuation Homework:

I don't like cherryade		my sister is only three.
I got 10/10 in my spelling test		the garden was carpeted in leaves.
Rover can't eat chocolate	;	I studied very hard.
It was autumn		I can't speak French or Italian either.
My eldest brother is sixteen		I much prefer lemonade.
I can't speak Spanish		it is poisonous to dogs.

1. I don't like cherryade; I much prefer lemonade.

2. _____

3. _____

4. _____

5. _____

6. _____

Homework

Look through your class reader. Find three examples of a sentence that uses a semi-colon.

Semi-colons

Write a School Report for a Year 4 pupil you have taught.
Will you write about the teacher's pet or the class clown?
What will you write about?
How will you tell the truth and still be polite?

Name: **Date:**

Know Moor County Primary School

General:

Punctuation for Parenthesis

Think about...
Why do people write down recipes?
How do these often look on the page?
Why are step by step instructions important?
Why are numbers, letters or Roman numerals often used?
What might happen to a recipe if they weren't used?

Guided

You are a wizard writing out a new spell.

How would it look? What headings and sub-headings might it include? What other text features might you see on the page? Why do you think these would be included? Make a list with a partner.

Once done, find another pair and compare your ideas. Then answer the questions on page 61.

Independent

You want to make a spider to scare your irritating brother or sister.

On your own, with a partner or in a small group; complete the task sheet provided to you by your teacher on page 62.

Once finished, cut off the homework task to take home with you for further practice.

Extension

You are a milliner teaching an apprentice how to make hats for a children's party. Complete the task sheet on page 63.

Once done, choose your favourite design and make it following your instructions.

Answers

1 1 [2] 3 4 5

2 1 2 3 4 [5]

3 For this spell you will need (A) milk, (B) stardust and (C) 3 whiskers.

Homework

- No specific answers are required for this task, though teachers should check that their illustrated guide includes at least one example of punctuation for parenthesis, as well as seeing how well Harry the hairy spider has been made.

Remember...
We use **parenthesis** to separate numbers or letters at the start of a list. When the list is inside a sentence, we use full parenthesis in order to enclose each number or letter.

Punctuation for Parenthesis

Spell Bound

A classic spell that will enable you to change yourself into a furry, purry feline.

Ingredients:
1. The blossom of a Tiger Lily
2. The chrysalis of a caterpillar
3. Three whiskers plucked from a sea lion
4. Stardust taken from the constellation of Leo
5. Milk (preferably whole and not semi-skimmed)

The Magic Words:
Abracadabra, Ali-Shazat.
Make this old wizard*
turn into a cat!

*Witch if you are a sorceress.

Instructions:
To prepare for morphification you will need to (1) Chop the petals of the Tiger Lily and crush the chrysalis into a fine powder, (2) add this mixture to the milk, (3) stir with the whiskers thirteen times anti-clockwise, (4) sprinkle over a generous pinch of the stardust and 5 pour the mixture over your head while saying the magic words.

Note:
The colour of your coat will be determined by the colour of your own hair. Don't expect to be a Ginger Tom if your golden locks have long since turned snow white.

Look at this list of ingredients and answer the questions below.

1 Which ingredient is missing its punctuation for parenthesis?

  1   2   3   4   5

1 mark

2 Which instruction is missing its punctuation for parenthesis?

  1   2   3   4   5

1 mark

3 Which of these sentences below is punctuated correctly? Tick one box.

For this spell you will need (A) milk, B) stardust, C) 3 whiskers. ☐

For this spell you will need A) milk (B) stardust and (C) 3 whiskers. ☐

For this spell you will need (A) milk, (B) stardust, (C) 3 whiskers. ☐

For this spell you will need (A) milk, (B) stardust and (C) 3 whiskers. ☐

1 mark

Punctuation for Parenthesis

Put these instructions in the correct order. Don't forget to add your punctuation for parenthesis. You can choose numbers, letters or Roman numerals.

Harry the Hilarious Hairy Spider!	
	Cut out the centre of each large circle so that you now have a pair of doughnut-like rings.
	Placing both rings on top of each other, take your ball of wool and tie one end of the wool tightly around the rings.
	Take a long piece of wool (so you can hang it) and tie it tightly in a double knot so that all the woollen loops come together to form a pom pom. Once secure, you can then remove the cardboard.
	Draw some eyes and fangs (or a smile depending upon what type of spider you are making) onto your sticky labels. Colour in, cut out and stick on.
	Hey presto! You can now say hello to your very own Harry the hilarious hairy spider.
	Wind the wool around the two rings until it is covered in one continuous layer of wool. The thicker the layer, the hairier your spider will be.
	Take your cardboard and draw two large circles on it. Draw a smaller circle in the centre of each one.
	Scrunch your four pipe cleaners together before pushing them through the woollen pom pom. When secure, bend each pipe cleaner in half to form two legs.
	When done, carefully cut along the outer edge of the ball making sure you don't cut through the middle.
	Collect your items: cardboard, wool, a pair of scissors, four pipe cleaners and a couple of sticky labels.

Homework

Try making Harry the spider. Follow the instructions carefully and see how big a spider you can make. Once made, create an illustrated step by step guide on how to make Harry.

Punctuation for Parenthesis

You are a milliner (or hat maker to me and you). Write an illustrated guide on how to design and make a simple hat for a children's fancy dress party. What kind of hat will it be? What materials will you need? What will you need to do first? What will your next step be? How will you decorate your hat?

Name: **Date:**

How to Make a Hat

You will need:

About the author of this book

John Murray

John Murray is a recognised specialist in developing children's reading skills through interactive and kinaesthetic approaches.

Since graduating from the University of North Wales in 1997, with a Bachelor of Education degree in English and Communication, John has taught in a wide variety of schools and situations. His experience includes teaching pupils with complex language difficulties and in communities where English is not the first language. Such challenging experiences have inspired John to create innovative new approaches to the teaching and learning of Literacy; developing techniques, ideas and methods that benefit all in the classroom.

Having created the best selling *Reading Explorers* series – highly regarded in schools across Britain and sold worldwide, he balances his teaching with his work as an independent writer and lectures on how to develop key literacy skills in leading colleges and universities. He also provides both internal and external training courses for schools.

For more information regarding resources and training from John Murray visit: **www.johnmurraycpd.co.uk**